GROWING UP

Visiting the Dentist

Charlotte Guillain

Raintree

www.raintreepublishers.co.uk
Visit our website to find out
more information about
Raintree books.

To order:
☎ Phone 0845 6044371
🖹 Fax +44 (0) 1865 312263
🖳 Email myorders@raintreepublishers.co.uk

Customers from outside the UK please telephone +44 1865 312262

Raintree is an imprint of Capstone Global Library
Limited, a company incorporated in England and Wales
having its registered office at 7 Pilgrim Street, London,
EC4V 6LB – Registered company number: 6695582

Text © Capstone Global Library Limited 2011
First published in hardback in 2011
The moral rights of the proprietor have been asserted.

Edited by Dan Nunn, Rebecca Rissman, and Sian Smith
Designed by Joanna Hinton-Malivoire
Picture research by Elizabeth Alexander
Originated by Capstone Global Library Ltd
Printed and bound in China by Leo Paper
Products Ltd

ISBN 978 1 406 22052 0 (hardback)
15 14 13 12 11
10 9 8 7 6 5 4 3 2 1

British Library Cataloguing in Publication Data
Guillain, Charlotte.
  Visiting the dentist. – (Growing up)
  1. Dental clinics–Pictorial works–Juvenile literature.
  2. Dentistry–Pictorial works–Juvenile literature.
  I. Title II. Series

617.6-dc22

Acknowledgements
We would like to thank the following for permission to
reproduce photographs: Alamy p. 19 (© Lisa Eastman);
Corbis pp. 5 (© Wolfgang Flamisch), 6 (© Bill Varie/
Somos Images), 7 (© Stefanie Grewel), 13 (© Paul
Burns), 23 glossary receptionist (© Bill Varie/Somos
Images); Getty Images p. 8 (Indeed/Digital Vision);
iStockphoto p. 12 (© emre ogan); Photolibrary pp. 4
(ERproductions Ltd/Blend Images), 15 (Image Source),
16, 20 (Medicimage), 21 (UpperCut Images), 23
glossary tooth decay (Medicimage); Shutterstock pp. 9
(© kristian sekulic), 10 (© Bork), 11 (© Bogac Erguvenc),
14 (© Dmitriy Shironosov), 17 (© Jozsef Szasz-Fabian),
18 (© Monkey Business Images), 23 glossary filling (©
Jozsef Szasz-Fabian), 23 glossary probe (© Bork), 23
glossary X-ray (© Bogac Erguvenc), 23 glossary fluoride
(© Anton Prado photo).

Front cover photograph of a dentist and patient
reproduced with permission of Corbis (© Bill Varie/
Somos Images). Back cover photographs of a mirror
reproduced with permission of Shutterstock (© Bork),
and a mask reproduced with permission of iStockphoto
(© emre ogan).

We would like to thank Neesha Patel for her invaluable
help in the preparation of this book.

Every effort has been made to contact copyright
holders of material reproduced in this book. Any
omissions will be rectified in subsequent printings if
notice is given to the publisher.

Contents

Some words are shown in bold, **like this**.
You can find them in the glossary on page 23.

Why do I need to go to the dentist?

teeth

You need strong, healthy teeth to eat your food.

It is important to keep your teeth healthy.

You go to the dentist to check your teeth are healthy and growing well.

The dentist can also help you if your teeth hurt or get knocked out.

What happens when I arrive?

When you get to the dentist's you speak to the **receptionist**.

The receptionist will ask some questions and there might be some forms to fill in.

Then you sit quietly in the waiting room until the dentist is ready to see you.

There are often toys and books for you to look at.

What happens when I go in?

When you go into the dentist's room the dentist or a dental nurse will meet you.

You might like to take your mum or dad into the room with you.

The dentist will ask you to sit in a special chair that moves up and down.

There is a big light over the chair to help the dentist see inside your mouth.

What is the dentist's equipment for?

probe

mirror

The dentist uses a tool called a **probe** to look at your teeth.

The dentist uses a special mirror to see all around your teeth.

The dentist also has an **X-ray** machine.

This machine takes pictures that show the inside of your body.

Why does the dentist wear a mask and gloves?

The dentist wears a mask over his or her nose and mouth.

The mask stops germs from the dentist's nose and mouth spreading to you.

The dentist wears gloves when he or she touches your mouth.

This is to stop germs on his or her hands spreading to you.

What does the dentist need to check?

The dentist looks at your teeth to make sure they are healthy.

The dentist will use the mirror and **probe** to check your teeth.

The dentist will also count your teeth.

He or she might also give you advice on how to look after your teeth.

What happens if there is a problem?

tooth decay

If you have toothache there might be a problem with your teeth.

Sometimes people get toothache when they have **tooth decay**.

filling

If there is a hole in a tooth, the dentist may need to give you a **filling**.

A filling fills up the hole and stops the tooth decaying any more.

Will going to the dentist hurt?

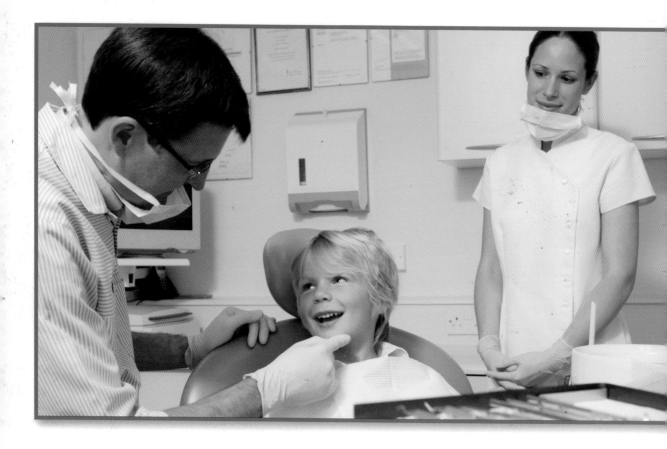

A normal check-up won't hurt at all.

It might just feel a little strange as the dentist looks around your mouth.

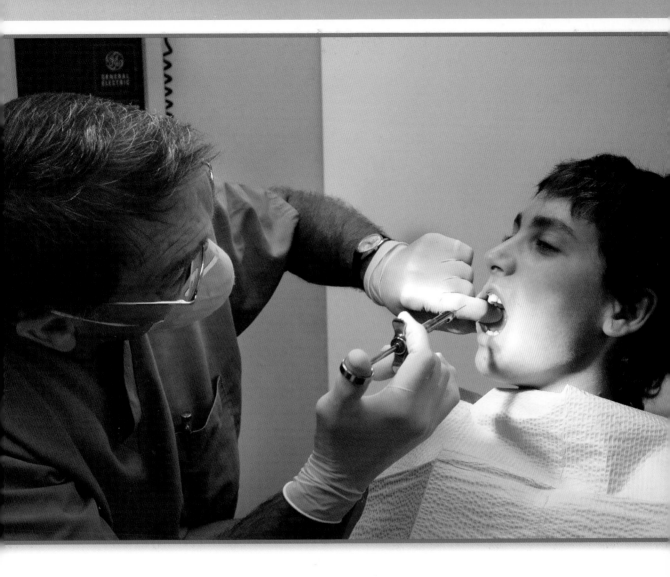

If you need a **filling**, the dentist might give you an injection.

This might prick a little but it does not hurt for long.

What happens at the end of a check-up?

When the dentist has finished checking your teeth, you can rinse your mouth out.

You can spit the mouthwash out into a bowl by the chair.

The dentist might give you a sticker or a new toothbrush.

Your mum or dad might make your next appointment with the **receptionist**.

How to look after your teeth

- Brush your teeth with **fluoride** toothpaste twice every day. Always brush your teeth before you go to bed.

- Try to drink milk or water. Too much fruit juice, squash, or fizzy drinks can hurt your teeth.

- Don't eat too many sweets or other sugary foods.

- If you want a snack, have a piece of fruit.

- Milk and milk foods such as cheese help to make your teeth strong.

Picture glossary

 filling material the dentist uses to fill a hole in a tooth

 fluoride chemical used in most toothpastes which helps to keep teeth healthy

 probe tool that dentists use to find out if teeth have holes

 receptionist person sitting at a desk near the entrance of a building, who meets people and tells them where to go

 tooth decay damage and holes in teeth

 X-ray photograph of inside the body

Find out more

Books

Going to the Dentist, Anna Civardi and Stephen Cartwright (Usborne, 2005)

Healthy Teeth, Angela Royston (Heinemann Library, 2003)

Investigate: Teeth, Charlotte Guillain (Heinemann Library, 2008)

Websites

Find out more information about taking care of your teeth:
http://kidshealth.org/kid/stay_healthy/body/teeth.html

Index